APPEARANCES

Appearances

Michael Collins

Saddle Road Press

Appearances
© 2017 by Michael Collins

Saddle Road Press
Hilo, Hawai'i
www.saddleroadpress.com

All rights reserved. No part of this book may be reproduced or transmitted in any form or by any means without written permission of the author.

Author photograph by Annie Kim
Cover image and book design by Don Mitchell

ISBN 978-0-9969074-5-3
Library of Congress Control Number: 2017948381

Contents

Appearances	9

I

Poem for a Predator	13
Pluviophilia	14
Vision	15
Reflection	16
Winter	17
landscape with figure and ground	18
Creation	19
Before Day Breaks	20
Fall	21
Circles	22
Neighbors	23
High Tide	24
Genesis	25

II

Esse in Anima	29
Low Tide	30
Lines	31
Communion	32
Metamorphoses	33
Apostasy	34
Dead Fish	35
Shells	36
Imagination	38
Sunrise	39
Images	40
between worlds	41
Nature	42

III

Portraits of Soul	45
Still Life	46
Tradition	47
Myth	48
Harbor Mandala	49
Seawall	50
The Sacrosanct Mallard of Mamaroneck Harbor	51
Rendering	52
Fog	53
Composition	54
Ars Poetica	56
Negatives of Soul	57

IV

Eclogues	61

V

Epiphany	71
Mother's Day	72
Matins	73
Katabasis	74
Snowstorm	75
Prayer	76
Constitutional	77
Morning	78
Self-Portrait	79
After High Tide	80
Acknowledgements	81
About the Author	83

There is another world, and it is this one.

Appearances

Soul never presents in its own shape:
purr of current flowing to remain,
breeze across a cheek, the hawk's

figure on the wind, imprint: beak in a rabbit
corpse, the vision's quick breath, impalement:
sun in hair, defying laws and powers: clouds

making mortals imagine horses
become horses: horses become gods: visions
incarnate, transforming flesh: bodies becoming

visions, passions, exhausting bodies into existence—
and then, and then— the meteor, shellshock: Soul
can only stalk sunfaces from their shadows,

the past, never—arrow— struck: similes bleed out
into metaphors, conjoined, conceiving: time unified
with form, annulling both: the world

a dew, glistening into the daytime; entropy claims
every dawn, leaving us wishing we could gasp
again the last: the remembered—imagined—

experienced—the body where breath was
twin: Each newly formed apocalypse recreates
the loss of wholeness to escape it: Some proclaim

the whole revelation a dream; others forge
moral fortresses to punish every loss; those lost
beyond strictures still must live: Lay down

sky, wind, unbreathable depths, the fled
in graves of language before unimaginable,
almost enough to imagine

wandering on.

I

Poem for a Predator

Do you hate me or crave me past sanity?
Either causes the pleasant and polite
to wolf down
         others' lives. I need to leave,

take an aimless wander by the harbor,
its field freckled with pairs of sunbathers,
a circle
      of blithe retirees in lawn chairs

gabbing and smoking and ranting and laughing,
a man lobbing a ball for a Labrador, kneeling
to bear
      hug him when he gasps it back—

My soul has no use for this human kindness
today, wants to gaze through the surface
of this
      water, the overcast sky's mirror,

look with her violent eye through the placid
black artifice edged with grey wavelets,
imagine herself back
         home into that world:

Creatures preying on one another
for no *good* reason, only instinct, living
and dying out
        of neither shame nor abhorrence.

Pluviophilia

Uncorpsed from my logical crusade
in the so-called other world of myth,
I'm human enough to admit it:
I failed to subject emanations,

gods and muses, nymphs and satyrs and
the sun, the figured stars, the winds, the
titans, Tartarus, Olympus, all
of the people becoming trees and

crows and flowers, lions, monsters,
some even gods, some just immortal
dust, the impossible Underworld—
all to the utterly tenuous

totalidoxy I thought I was
seeking to verify you exist.

I suppose this is all for the best.
Infallible ideas tend to lead to holy wars.
And, what with me having no army,
such conquests would tend to end poorly.

I bet I wouldn't like it either
if you were so busy concocting
Michaelologies comprehensive
enough to crush the breath from my lungs

that you withheld this delicate rain,
in which the world that fled my theories
returns to glisten, delighting skin,
the earth a cradle made of water,

being-in-soul the only knowledge.
You are present, therefore the cosmos.

Vision

Stopped dead in my tracks: a perfect half clam
shell, purples and violets woven at the bottom,
yielding to a flesh-like alabaster
where it deepens, curling through the middle:

an almost human ear, strange oblong shape,
thin pastel blue veins tendering their way
up its whole length to a tiny bright lobe,
echo of where once a tiny creature

connected this hollow with its mirror—
Death has been here; can I forgive this,
offer you again what I call my voice
to say, soul of beak and stone, wind and waves,

Every fragment contains its own wholeness;
for this moment, it is only beautiful?

Reflection

I wanted to promulgate it a great violation.
But when I quit pretending to be the harbor's

righteous witness, I see it is just
a little spill— Someone must have slipped

while filling a gas tank— My soul compels me
to take in this translucent painting before me,

circles of beige and grey mixed with light
metallic blue crescents, slivers of clear water

curling through the colors, a tiny child's fingers
first grasping the thumb of the unfathomable

giant from whom he'd fought toward that awful light.

Winter

I imagine I could walk across the harbor.
Water whispers through just a few unfrozen pools.
The waves have transmigrated to the bright, white shore,
rhythmic gusts plucking swirlings of sun dancing snow,

sweeping them over smooth banks while tickling my face—
The poet remembers a time before making
forms of words to reflect nature's consciousness, back
to his snowangeling child incarnation—

The no longer green swamp grass cannot really be
deceased, just this season's brown version of itself;
precipitation has repainted every tree

with shimmering leaves, creations recreating
one another, being recreated, patient
place where I see as my soul, world rebuilding me.

LANDSCAPE WITH FIGURE AND GROUND

a host of sparrows beak
      the harbor grass wave
            after wave alighting away
                  with every step i take
            toward them the water
      displays a stillness
normally the shore's
      property undisrupted
           by birds nor the light
                mist i remember hoping
            images born in dreams
      would give birth to a future
for me alone *now*
      i walk here alive and seeing
            things and their deepness
                together again everything seems
            to have inverted the universe
      i once thought within me
now the one i traverse
      world and psyche alive
           in the other the rain came
                without notice stroking the body
            of water it was once
      again i am a small boy
gazing at my childhood
      lake now far away
           on the sands of the bed
                my ancestors' ashes dance

Creation

The fleshy snowflakes
twisting blissfully down
through the faint breeze

seem to have been made
in the image of the paperweight
I would gaze at as a child,

a tiny half world upended
in beautiful flurry, set down at will
by a suddenly gigantic hand

to quiet and awe the eye.

Before Day Breaks

Just ahead of dawn the swirling mist
revels the souls of trees back down

to their native, flattened images,
unified on the water's surface

before they return to daily figures
on birdsong and matins of frogs.

Hands to the sky and toes just brushing
over the water, like stones thrown by children,

the nymphs skip quickly through the haze,
barely glimpsed, the myths live again. Soon,

the sun will again seem each thing separate.

Fall

I am one   of the leaves   floating on the harbor

    this morning, detached   from mother, branch,   roots, ripples

holding me, dancing,   delighted, spinning   into decomposition,

    grateful   blissfully mingled   with terrified.

The wavelets spin   me for seconds,   forever; I

    embrace the gracious   freedom I never saw   coming. I sink in;

I allow it   to sink in: This was the best   year of my life.

Circles

I made myself pause for just that second.)
I could have chucked my travel mug

at this nimrod spitefully gunning his truck
to slush me as I walked in the street,

cautious footsteps avoiding the as-of-yet
unshoveled sidewalks, slipping on slick snow,

heatedly thinking, *Of course, this sadist
would prey on my innocent wish*

to see the summer harbor winter. (I had
been waiting like kids for Christmas,

marshmallowing in snowsuits, falling
into softness, the snow awaiting

the shape of my play as I arrive
and squish across the yet untrodden lawn,

beaming back at the sun to see the way
the storm has transformed the water

into the ice rink we once ankle-bent around,
slowly orbiting in the crisp new breeze,

each winter again the same adventure.

Neighbors

Boats and their attendant people form
rows in the harbor, yet ducks continue

duckly practices between them or idle blithely
along the seawall even when I wander near.

Somehow they've learned we harbor pilgrims
look at them without seeing dinner. I wish

more people could be more like this duck,
with his head turned backwards, napping,

beak tucked between feathers, grey and purple, here
and there a speckle of red, opening one eye as I pass

and, seeing merely another creature
who means him no harm, drifts back to sleep—

though the swan down in the sea grass sunning
arches his long white neck, stares dead at me.

Foghorns bloody murder until I leave.

High Tide

When I arrived today,   black clouds were nighting;
the harbor had changed   its shape, the seawall
flooded in its lower places, the wooden swing a levitating island.

Minnows silver here and   there, dreams through the sleeping,
swaying green grass blades   gone under once again.
Quick little lightnings   of the world's slumbering mind,

tiny oracles, what holds   the future? Feeling I've hidden
from my wild soul   behind smiling masks—
will it end? And if so how   will I escape eternity this time?

Genesis

by the water in the summer
i welcome in near ecstasy

your cool fingers brushing
sweat from my forehead

your breath whispering
conch songs over my ears

the force of your greater
being pressed against me

i will not release you

winter seems a nightmare
wind whipping through

as if to persuade me
from delicate images

of ever gentle immortals
exquisitely dreaded

immanent expressions
angel i know you *here* in flesh

until you bless me

II

Esse in Anima

We are each ourselves at the harbor:
Runners run, readers read, children play,

I wander within myself within
the world, nothing is even wrong

with the distant cars in their straight lines,
driving from lot to lot as people

walk between ducks who simply sit
in the sun—I have given my eyes

too deeply to the breeze this morning;
I nearly stepped on one of them.

From how it looked, he would have let me.

Low Tide

The tide ebbs; bed turns
venture out excitedly

lines into the current
the secrets the absent

run balls from the nearby
remnants of someone's party,

puddles left behind, stones
open clams' shells

into shore, and children
to the new boundary, casting

unseen; my eye takes in
water has exposed: Home

diamond and aluminum memories,
mingle with sea grass, small green

dug into the mud, peeking
lined up like tombstones.

Lines

We've divided   the harbor
in the only proper,   logical way:
In an enclosed   semi-circle

in the shallows,   children squeal
and dive, shoot   water from guns
into water. Out   in the cove

boats with names   rest, waiting
like hearth gazing   heroes anxious
for adventures.   Beyond them:

The deep world   we can't see
on land, can   only dream, imagine—
where we may   drown nonetheless.

Communion

Two old men in fleeces and ball caps
cast minnowed lines from each side of the dock—

Then suddenly one is the grandfather
who first brought his friend to this place

long ago, before time; the one
with the taut line, transfigured with awe,

five-year-olds a miraculous flashing
across the water's surface, towels it gently,

polishing silver the night before Easter,
treasures it into a *Stop&Shop* bag

that hangs from the chain link fence thrashing.

Metamorphoses

The harbor ice has chipped, shuffled, reformed
into a long, smooth slab of beige and black
granite;
                  ducks have transformed into pigeons
for winter, their feathers pastel paintings;

the snowsuited woman kneeling to pray
remakes the lone, cold beach into a temple;

these three gulls body surfing on wind waves
can only be shrieking with toddlers' glee:

My eyes play at tracing their gusts' shapes as

another drops a clam down on the ice,
scurries after it, captures his treasure,

again, again, again, again, forever,

a tiny child's complete enthrallment
with throwing and clasping a brand new ball.

Apostasy

Which unmitigated aesthetic wizard,
with obviously too much free time,
fitted wind socks with wings, clever eyes and beaks,

and posted them all around the harbor,
a flock of post-Icarian nonsense,
soaring out to their tethers' ends sunward?

What was deficient in the Avian-
Americans already peopling this shore?
Don't these inverted birders know

I come here when I fear my soul
has fled forever so she will see me
through the eyes of gulls returning

from the water, swans craning backwards?
Can't they see I need her to display,
in the strange mirrors of this haven,

each of the parts of myself I've forgotten?

Dead Fish

In the end it was my fault
for thinking I could simply wander
here, naïve, Edenic among creatures yet

unnamed, never smelling that stench
demarcating a new place, seeing them
whole, desiccated, lying on the low tide

shore, picked at by birds, sliced
by engines, hanging impossibly from the sun
dried inner sea- wall, never

asking the locals their name: *Mossbunker,*
a greasy baitfish, no good *at all when too many die,*
it stinks, listening to the emanations of causes:

a spill, landscaping fertilizer, deoxygenated
water, suffocation, imagining the scene
an apocalyptic slaughter, a poisonous snake

eating its own tail, to express my innocent's
horror at discovering their bodies, the shame
of the child I had been, walking

here, daily stumbling upon tiny mysteries, as if
I would never see that first image, the lone
survivor slowing, turning on his back, his mouth out

into the air, swimming upside down,
spiraling, circling, finally springing from his home—
and hear myself think *Look,* *the fish is playing.*

Shells

The same thunderstorm that pummeled

        the seamless ice over the harbor

into a gathering of fragments

        has left the lawn a chain of inland lakes

where a paddling of ducks splash and wade.

        In warm months we visitors strolled

beside their lounging, downy bodies.

        I'm so alone here today in the cold,

my mind can marry the icy harbor

        and cloudy sky within one image,

sharing the same misty interwoven blues,

        greys: Surely, this world is the mirror

the soul shows me to be seen, that I shutter

        for protection. The ducks scurry, plunge

all at once into a small pool

    between sheets of ice; a gull hovers

redoubtably before releasing

    the clam it cradles in its claws

all the way back down to the waiting land,

    a crash, and all certainty's shattering.

Imagination

My steps once traced the harbor's actual shore.
I listened intently to its images.
But January's path is frozen.

seventeen men left Mamaroneck

I must keep my eyes down on my boots,
hopscotching the tracks of soles' impressions
captured during their freezing. My mind wanders

seventeen soldiers in the great war

within; my journey turns circular: two
asymmetrical basins round into one,
seamless, faultless: unfractured world of forms and

seventeen characters nameless in histories

muses: gods war with titans, myths nymph
waters, constellate heavens— I look up briefly;
my mind walks into the harbor's open mouth,

seventeen boys in a trench I imagine

into the Underworld, sky, ocean: cosmos
emanating before me, inside me eternity
merely breathing. I return from this unmarchable

seventeen sons never came back

place where the temporal opens to the depths,
having arrived at a strange memorial,
alone in the snow like the harbor's sentinel:

seventeen names on a metal plaque

on a cannon aimed right at that open space.

Sunrise

Morning. Alone   by the water. Walking   through dreams seeming

to mean nothing   in this waking. Water still   as ever. Absent

the slightest   breeze. Little   birds skittering

over the tiny harbor   bed islands,   revealed, abandoned

only by low tide,   as if they fear   disturbing what I wish

into this picture   perfect mirror: Two   suns. One still

ascending, beginning   to sweat   my skin, the other

trapped by water   on its surface,   an image burning

without heat. A nebula   of tiny bugs   claims my sight.

Can't reason   these worlds back   together.

Images

Someone took one of the titanic   vessels that dream
in the harbor out to the deep waters   to go fishing. Now

large fish carcasses litter the shore;   cleaned skin
floats on the surface like wet paper;   large, white stoic heads

still bob, singing the wavelets' quiet   lullabies. The water
will pull back if I *imagine* washing   my hands. Clouds

of tiny fish minnow around   the guillotined, quick-
silvery as those dreams wakened   away with the alarm,

much luckier than those I thought   archetypal, so universal
they simply must have meant something   justifying dissection,

consuming—so beautiful they could only have been entirely about me.
These days I look *out* at the water; still   at times like these

so little seems to have changed   in how I see.

BETWEEN WORLDS

muddy fiddler crabs
scurrying about with
onesided giant claws
born into cycles
emerging at low tide
in the muck
hungry returning
to deeper burrows
instinct is their schedule

behind me
workmen smashing
metal on metal
they live by
building carnival rides
to cast quick lightning
wild down childspines
always a newness
it's that time again

Nature

Halfway down the pier into the harbor,
three chain link fences,

wooden slats woven through the openings,
haphazardly block the path.

A sign is posted: *County pier closed. Enter
at your own risk.*

Behind it the walkway continues, between chains
joined to posts guiding

out to a darkened street light, echoes of times
when people ventured

to the edge, looked down into that unfathomable,
mysterious mirror. Now

it is overgrown—wild, sharp-leafed plants and tall grass.
A dragonfly menaces

the curious, gatekeeper to this rough, slumbering
sanctuary where nature

redreams itself, within human construction. I look in;
I do not trespass.

III

Portraits of Soul

First toy plane wobbles on breezes.
There's a charge for the beach again.

The harbor's a flurry of work:
juggernaut mowers crop the lawn,
bushes are trimmed, the sand is combed
and brushed away from the walkways,
a team sweeps and lines the clay courts,
boats bustle with gossip and cleaning—

Spring is here! This place must prepare

for people; forms must be in things
and beings ever shaping space,
and these eyes that we have seen through,
must return to their visions' graves:

Make something of what can't exist.

Still Life

The wastes' shades gather together
against the seawall, ghostly

fingers of tan and olive witnessing
themselves in and through one another,

with each breeze the transparent canvas
bearing a new figureless mystery,

on its surface a duck nibbling
amidst the beautiful, doodling oils.

Tradition

Today, before the fireman statue
who faces away from the harbor,
the living observe a remembrance:

Pressed formal uniforms are worn,
anthem saluted, wreaths presented,
each solemnity tenderly performed—

Each generation begs for ritual
to relinquish, to replace— How
did this rite's author properly punctuate

lives of terminating infernos?
I once wandered here without conceiving
poems, sparking, ashed onto the page,

read, perhaps, by eyes still
mysteries to me, confession taking
place, almost like in the old world,

before the communion, last rites.

Myth

walking until he becomes
        the verb itself, until
                this place becomes
        the book, until
the book silences striving
        and fear, becomes
                a home, becomes
        a body, walking,
a body, for moments, walking,
        timeless, a walking
                body creating
        a home, a home
creating the mind that creates
        the home it walks
                through, creating
        a world that creates
the creator, walking until
        the jagged harbor is
                a circle, walking until
        he is himself, until
he is also the self
        he is not, until
                he creates the creator
        who walks with him
beside the quiet
        water, the harbor, only
                the harbor

HARBOR MANDALA

      i have come to you harbor
      this morning after a nightmare
      absconded only its anxious
      wake still within me

beyond the shoreside minnows   demanding i apprehend
below the gulls perched on buoys   the amorphous dream
the small boat trolling depthward   subject it to reason
to beg for what it cannot see   force it to signify something

      your surface a canvas
      where the cloud muted sun
      paints abstract patterns
      deep blues shadowed with greys

whatever i thought i was   i could have come empty
to see was not this   silently greeted a friend
wind brushing across   opened my eyes
your skin creating visions   invited you into my soul

      ducks nap silently
      in the oak shade i wander by
      my sandals quacking with
      each step on my way home

Seawall

I walk along the mortared stones
designed to contain high tide.

White flecks speckle their surface;
once they were clams' shells cast down

to be shattered by hungry gulls
with eyes and instincts and no words

to name an act *murder*. Nature, pure
transformation. Instantly

the world is only this cycling;
there is nothing
                    I must render.

The Sacrosanct Mallard of Mamaroneck Harbor

Listen, Jesus, it wasn't my idea
for this mallard to stand on the dock,
stretching his wings out all crucifixiony.

Hell, I thought he was a crow.

I had to ask a guy on a boat the true name
of my enigma, which led to his description:
how the birds alight and circle, dive down,

transmigrate the water's plane, return,

beaks full of fish. The poet in my head
extolled, *Holy Post-modern iconography,
Boat Guy! That story has a Christ*

image crushing the life from another!

Surely some revelation's at hand—again!
I thanked the butt crack he turned back to me,
scampered off quickly to epiphanize,

lest you revert to just some bird.

Rendering

This water did not call   itself *harbor,*
yet here ships   slumber, people imagine
books   into breezes, children

splash breath   back into the shallows,
one mad cackle   beckoning another.
And I worship what I cannot   control:

Can't shape the way   the hurricane turned
sky into a twin   ocean, tore from the earth
like *saplings*   trees a hundred

years of rain had raised; seemingly   composed now,
these waters took   to land before the winds came,
flooding roads; some kids   drove their truck

into the new   pools, screaming deliriously,
over and over, up   and down the disappearing block,
each new spray of   danger a fresh forever.

Fog

Harbor and fog duet onto a canvas,

        the sun rendering itself, muted

blues antiphoning with an unbrushable

        orange framed in tangerine haze,

lonely red and white *Lifeguard Off*

        Duty sign, twenty feet of sand wafting

down to the water, vague beachwalkers'

        shapes ghosting along in the beyond.

As the mist lifts, the dock, with its clam shell

        searching children and fisherman fathers,

drifts like a picture quietly rising

        in a darkroom; a mallard performs

what I name a dance on the fence, outstretching

        its wings, shimmying side to side.

Do I have a right to these images,

        to lyric the space between me and

my vision? The landscape remains

        in every way unchanged.

Composition

On the near side of the harbor:
an amoeba of three-year-olds
blobbing around the lawn, chasing

a ball none of them can possess,
undisciplined as the pitch they squeal
alive, sidestepping trees and bushes,

playing something that will grow,
with time and training sharpen
into soccer. On the far side:

perceptions fixed with conviction,
as gleaming jerseys brandish numbers,
teammates kneeling, circling coaches,

dividing team into positions,
reviewing duties, strategies,
sizing up the opposition,

nets fixed to goals, corner flags placed,
straight white lines chalked upon the grass.
As if the landscape had no options,

split into the pages needed
for each of the untold stories
some stranger has cast to tell themselves.

I keep thinking; it bothers me:
both sides' backs turned to the harbor
between them, though it is all

either can see of their other version—
or the future, when telling stories
will come to substitute for playing.

Every reflection deserves what it gets.

Ars Poetica

All week an odd shaped silhouette
against the sky, a bird conveying
branches up to the top of the flood lights
of the harbor's baseball diamond,

building a nest in which fledglings will learn
how to fly between two worlds. Hence,
for a moment, she seems my soul,
teaching me to perceive in this landscape

the shapes of psyche; then she is a bird
again, gliding on ametaphorical wind—
I must capture this transformation! I look up
once I have written the poem. She is gone.

Negatives of Soul

The school of herring
    feeding near the dock
        whorl around and
            through one another's
        paths, weaving what would be
    invisible tapestries
if they had a purpose
    beyond being, a cloud
        of mouths and fins
            silvering the overcast
        water, boundless, surrounded
    by succor I cannot see,
every one the ground
    and figure, each one
        the movement,
            only the circling,
        inhumanly patient, never
    waiting for the mortal
eye that sees them
    in this vision, no longer
        mine; it exists
            only insubstantially,
        only within them, only
    in this instant, desperate
to become *this*.

IV

Eclogues

I came to this harbor unconsciously.
Seeking a mother made of breeze and waves.

One of those sublime lies the soul will tell
to trick a depressed man up out of bed.

Even after I reasoned this was silly,
I still liked it here, so I wrote poems

to honor the landscape for its own sake,
lending my voice to the slumbering fiddler

crabs and their marshland and ducks and swans and clams,
feeling rather magnanimous, thank you.

As if nature were some place you visit,
some museum to nostalgia through—

unless the real world interjects a text.
There's nothing to fear or worship here, no

gods or oracles, nymphs, myths, underworlds.
Even if there were I couldn't see them

through this choppy, muddy water below
where I stand on a dock, holding a fence,

winds nearly knocking me over, screaming,
Listen, simple child, the storm is coming.

The harbor has flooded the lawn once again.
A newsman films this peculiar view, as if
it was the craft of our recent Nor'easter.
This happens each high tide; even I know that,

and I still ask locals names of plants and fish.
I know only the truth of what I've *seen*—
Sadly the same with those who'll watch this segment,
these images submerged within a *story*

much more compelling than some simple harbor,
from whose daily happenings it was crafted.
He will earn his check, make it through another
shot and narrative edited seamlessly

together, another knock out job well done.
Maybe his piece isn't even an untruth
he knew he was filming, his small transgression
unintended or simply venial, the lies

we all speak for smiles, titles, survival.
He asks to ask me a couple of questions.
I decline; he has no use for my response:
This is *only* water disregarding walls.

It does this whenever it wishes, rain, shine,
storm, apocalypse— *Water*, I know you
cannot rescue me from *this* world even if I could—
No. That's just another kind of production.

Best to walk here in the winter.
It comforts my eyes, focusing
solely on the wholly bright ground.

I've been mindfully setting down
feet on this soft, inviting snow;
I'm old enough to know I may

slip, be split
              open. Suddenly,
the water begins sneaking through
the seawall cracks—before long

overrun. The veil of snow turns
into a new pool of water,
growing, growing, though tomorrow

it will be ice, a month later,
the simple dirt and grass and sand
the tide has unveiled, the hidden

earth that was always waiting—

Listen, Death, I can live with you.
But, if they finally concur
to put down this wild creation
we've grown so damn tired of fearing
to make more things to throw away,
the timeless Reader will die too.

All I want to do is sit down in this pool,
repeat to whatever no-one is listening
the dread voice in my head that keeps telling me,

This poem will spark and flicker, dance and burn.

My balance once betrayed me in the snow.
Just like that, snapped both bones in my ankle.
My boots obscured how bad the fracture was,
and I had so many things still to do.

So, in a cliché of determined resolve,
I stood, literally tried to walk it off.

You trudge yourself down to the water
                                        to quiet the waves of your mind,
currently echoing the ways the world will turn
                                              into the cracked clam
shells you know are covered
                              under the snow. You see the seawall submerged
again today, a path descending down
                                to Hades; this time you say

There it is. That's death. But you continue
                                    around the harbor; the stones
resurface, only
                to descend, appear again ten paces later.
So then what are you saying? Seek
                        asylum in reincarnation?
No response but the sound of your feet,
                          a metronome of squishing snow

into footprints. It's impossible:
                      The soul is supposed to return
cleansed of memory; here you are
                          hearing your son ask that bird this morning,
What YOU doing, BIRD?,
                    repeating, cackling the eternal laughter
a toddler feeling silly emanates,
                recreating the world—

all now but the thought
                        of itself, the thought of how many toddlers
will after these last few months' killings
                            never again laugh, revulsion:

These two truths existing in one
                        world, one mind—and that being *your own*.
Then it just seems like death
                        really *must*, at last, be a meeting with God.

Or else *this* is just some pointless circle of nothing
                        ending nothing,
failing even to punctuate
                        one sentence of pointless suffering,
but walking back by the daily deluge,
                        you almost slip. Hidden ice!
The near fall frightens you
                        awake. You place yourself on a bench nearby

on the hill overlooking the flood; you see
                        how thin the water is,
never threatening to travel
                        on land for long.... Then you are dead!
Look down at the *whole* scene, *there*,
                        you, clomping home, set against white snow,
this person from whom, from a flashing
                        vantage, you sometimes seem free.

Today the fenced off path that once led
to the long dock between the harbor's
basins—no longer a place for
fantasy. I stop; the space begins:

> Its overgrown bushes, uncut grass,
> no longer the wildness of the deep
> psyche I once thought would heal me and
> the world back together with its fear-

less truth— Death will only be death, next
week, year, accident, cancer, shooting.
For a second I stop and wonder
why I'm even bothering to write.

> The dragonfly's ghost has had enough.
> *What were you ever writing for, death*
> *with your consciousness sarcophagized*
> *in more books on more shelves with more dust?*

Now, where the white and silver gull trolls
the freezing water, the chilling wind
searching my coat for my skin, the whole
frozen world, cowering, praying—

> Each moment of consciousness will die.
> Although it has always everywhered.
> This clam flying its gull overhead,
> neither meaning much of anything

unless I speak the voice that's saying
I forgive you for not containing
salvation, saying, *bless you, thank you*
for this song and this breath and this day.

Harbor, you used to make me feel beloved.
I was the special one then; you showed me
your secrets in images. Today: ice
floats on the surface, thin flake of dry skin.

Gentle ripples caress this quiet life;
no witness renders its relinquishment,
stolen frozen edges returned to home.
I shiver a need for this connection

to be more than a poem: eternal,
a body surviving the end of seasons.
My fear betrays me and I ask you, *Why
do any such quick embraces matter,*

collisions among unremembered names?
The landscape is all it has to say.

V

Epiphany

We made the crucifix a cross, imagined the actual
passion an afterthought, now deaf to Death's *Eloi, eloi*

lama—suspended yet, left palm split with goodness, the right
evil, dying, invisible blood giv'n for the victory

we Easter every single year, rehearsing holy notes for *Spring*!
For the snow had congregated every shade within its light,

reflected skyward; vanquished, it warms to its other
form, makes its pilgrimage to chthon. Color returns

to redeem each eye; by grace I may walk again
beside the harbor, yet I thirst to be ecstatic, hymn *All green!*

Surely the grass has arisen indeed! There *is* green here
and yellow, tan, and brown, all unjudged, for *Death* is *just*

the *end* of a perception. Then, new sights surprise once
again; they look quite similar to those lost: Believers' eyes look round

for endless seasons, the estranged eye straight ahead, next, next, the end.

Mother's Day

Your boats have returned, and picnics giggle
            from dock to beach like winter never happened;
rose blossoms anthem confetti across the lawn:

            Up the hill children's sports roar and squeal,
a volley strikes net off a corner kick,
            a dad sprouts from his squat at a base hit.

The games certainly seem to spring everyone green.
            The water beside me is already warming,
(Is it anticipating swimmers?)

            yet it has silently retreated toward the depths
because, (despite the fact that? while incidentally?)
            in the cold, quiet snow all of this fresh

joy again claims it has routed and banished,
            when I was alone here, it seemed I could hear
everything you would ever disclose.

Matins

Morning dusk. Can't sleep. Analyzing dreams.
Luckily, no one's down by the harbor,

so when the lone duck slices the water,
it literally is a single leaf
of paper tearing; the frost whitening
the still green grass is actually the mask

I wear into the plastic world, the fog
my destiny. The landscape permits this,

or the four-note birdsong in the darkness
up ahead could not become my mantra,
nor the obsidian water my still
fluid soul, the purple-grey mountain range

in the distance, the peaks I fear crossing
until I can see them back into clouds.

Katabasis

Death negates all
    specificity, compromises
        nothing: moral
            stature, journeys
        intended to end
  in victory, bonds
to those we cherish
    beyond reason— It is not
        an event; it is
            a perspective, growing
        slowly in each unique,
    separate sight, teaching
the way to see
    the highest
        tide trickling, fingers
            searching the sea-
        wall we imagine
  cannot be
transgressed, caressing
    the ground that wishes
        itself separate,
            the water a lens,
        entropic, transforming
    grains into the sand
bed it darkens, all
    the world
        again one
            eye.

Snowstorm

Sideways snow, feet soaked, coat penitent white,
growing certain my tombstone will snicker,
His shoes were too holey, his coat too thin,

as my mind's other *whatif*s encircle,
growling forth a chaos of ominous
corpsebirds from their imagined rabid maws.

I have to continue returning home.

The snow punishes me; I must look down
for my eyes' sanctuary; I relearn
my gait's percussion: place and step and place,
a heartbeat of movement, footsteps breathing—

In my feet's periphery, I'm surprised,

as I pass by this oddly calm water,
to see the ducks I'd thought flown south last week.

Prayer

Thank you for this sacred gull,
        swooping and circling through the noon
blue sky, so my eye could trace

        in his invisible wake
the shape of wind, soul through spirit,
        spirit through soul; it was thunderous

as it approached me—then transfigured
        its visage into a model plane's,
robbed me of the obvious god-

        image I apprehended, returned
the distance I call to you across,
        the between within which I listen.

Constitutional

Soon I will have no choice but to return
from my reprieve in the harbor breeze
to shuffling personas, fractions, splinters,
within which I hide in emails, meetings,

in between Facebooking and tweeting
as-if snippets of a Cubist Self-
Portrait. Yet inapprehendable
strolling moments such as these permit

the soul I live within to cruise
my body like a borrowed car
around our water, her mirror,
currently quite tranquil. I am

improving by and by at being
unconfined by duty, performance,
ambition, letting images *live*
in my eyes' quick forever. Today,

in fact, I've lasted almost half an hour.

Morning

The tiny ripples   did not begin   when I happened

upon them; the breeze   breezing them into   being does not symbolize

any Spirit uniting   us. Ducks cluster, scatter,   squawking like ducks,

not a performance   for my eyes; I'm only   a human being, taken

on a stroll with his soul   through soul as these souls   each live their creatures.

I've finished losing   the world I thought   I controlled; in the tiny light

flecks on delicate wavelets,   dawn and haven face   one another.

I'm reminded you speak   in visions, promising   prayers harmonize

deeper than soliloquies;   the water-   sparks' patternless dancing

duets its endpoints,   lineless pictograms, strange   succorous listening

to a language sung   in figures, one   I no longer have   to master.

Self-Portrait

The sun's warmth had once seemed to blend all waters
together in one harbor; winter's star lends

only light, and ice remembers that it is
a separate temporal being, slender life struggling

to live within the patient, quiet currents
as they give it shape, their movements keeping it

translucent; otherwise he could not look down
and see the dark waves palpitate their rhythms

underneath it, could not perceive this giant,
ancient heart through that impossible eyesight

the soul guides from here into its other world,
disclosed by what imagines to contain it.

After High Tide

The tide rose over
its confinement, now

from all of this harbor,
from all of the deeper

waters beyond, a small pool
lingers between the sea-

wall bricks and the sandy
dirt behind them on land.

A remnant, a remembrance,
a separate thing, already

losing itself, slowly being
absorbed by the new

body who holds it.

Acknowledgements

Many thanks to my wife and son for their love and support and to the friends and colleagues who spent time reading and discussing this manuscript, especially Joan Aleshire, Jayne Benjulian, Mary Lou Buschi, Annie Kim, Jennifer Franklin, Peg Alford Pursell, and JC Todd. I'm also grateful to Don Mitchell and Ruth Thompson at Saddle Road Press for their excellent work in bringing this book into being—and, of course, to the harbor that made it possible in the first place.

A portion of this manuscript appeared in the chapbook *Harbor Mandala*, published by Finishing Line Press. Thanks also to the publications below, in which the following poems from this collection first appeared.

"Sunrise" first appeared in *Lime Hawk*.
"Lines" first appeared in *Driftwood Press Literary Magazine*.
"Low Tide" first appeared in *Old Northwest Review*.
"between worlds" first appeared in *Spry Literary Journal*.
"Rendering" first appeared in *Waccamaw*.
"Seawall" first appeared as "Breakwater," in *Epigraph Magazine*.
"Neighbors" first appeared in *Constellations: A Journal of Poetry and Fiction*.
"Esse in Anima" first appeared in *The Inflectionist Review*.
"Ars Poetica" first appeared in *Marathon Literary Journal*.
"Before Day Breaks" first appeared in *Blotterature Literary Magazine*.
"Images" first appeared in *Grist Journal*.
"After High Tide" first appeared in *Broad River Review*.
"Fall," "Constitutional," and "Prayer" first appeared in *The Westchester Review*.

"The Sacrosanct Mallard of Mamaroneck Harbor," "Katabasis," and "Apostasy" first appeared in *Sequestrum*.

"Negatives of Soul" first appeared in *The Innisfree Poetry Journal*.

"Mother's Day" and "Epiphany" first appeared in *Homestead Review*.

"Poem for a Predator" first appeared in *RiverSedge*.

"genesis" first appeared in *Roanoke Review*.

"Pluviophilia," "Morning," and "harbor mandala" first appeared in *Modern Poetry Quarterly Review*.

"Vision" first appeared in *The Heartland Review*.

"Communion" first appeared in *The Adirondack Review*.

"Dead Fish" first appeared in *The Stickman Review*.

"Reflection" first appeared in *Reunion: The Dallas Review*.

About the Author

Michael Collins' poems have appeared in numerous journals and magazines, and he is also the author of the chapbooks *How to Sing when People Cut off your Head and Leave it Floating in the Water* and

Harbor Mandala and the full-length collection *Psalmandala*.

He teaches creative and expository writing at New York University and the Hudson Valley Writers' Center and is the Director of Studies at Why There Are Words Press.

Please visit Michael at www.notthatmichaelcollins.com

www.ingramcontent.com/pod-product-compliance
Lightning Source LLC
Chambersburg PA
CBHW020623300426
44113CB00007B/757